Yakima River

Yakima River

Steve Probasco

Frank Amato
PORTLAND

River Journal

Volume 2, Number 2, 1994

Steve Probasco is a full time writer/photographer living in Raymond, Washington. He grew up in Ellensburg, Washington and has fished the Yakima River for nearly 30 years. Steve's articles and photography appear regularly in several U.S., Canadian and British publications. Steve is the author of one book and one video on fly tying, with several other works in progress. He is a seminar speaker/fly tier for Ed Rice's International Sportsmen's Expositions, as well as a seminar speaker at the Federation of Fly Fishers International Fly Fishing Show.

◆

Acknowledgments

Many thanks to: Tim Irish, of Irish's Guide Service, for his expertise on the hatches and fishing found on the Yakima, and for being a friend on the river; Jim Cummins, from the Washington Department of Wildlife; the Bureau of Reclamation, Yakima Project Office; and the Northwest Power Plannning Council. All flies in the plate were provided by Spirit River, Inc. in Roseburg, Oregon (503) 440-6916. Thanks also to my dad, Cecil Probasco, for getting me hooked on fishing at an early age.

◆

Series Editor: Frank Amato

Design: Joyce Herbst
Photography: Steve Probasco
Fly Plate Photography: Jim Schollmeyer • Map: Tony Amato
Printed in Hong Kong
Softbound ISBN:1-878175-75-0, Hardbound ISBN:1-878175-76-9
(Hardbound Edition Limited to 600 Copies)

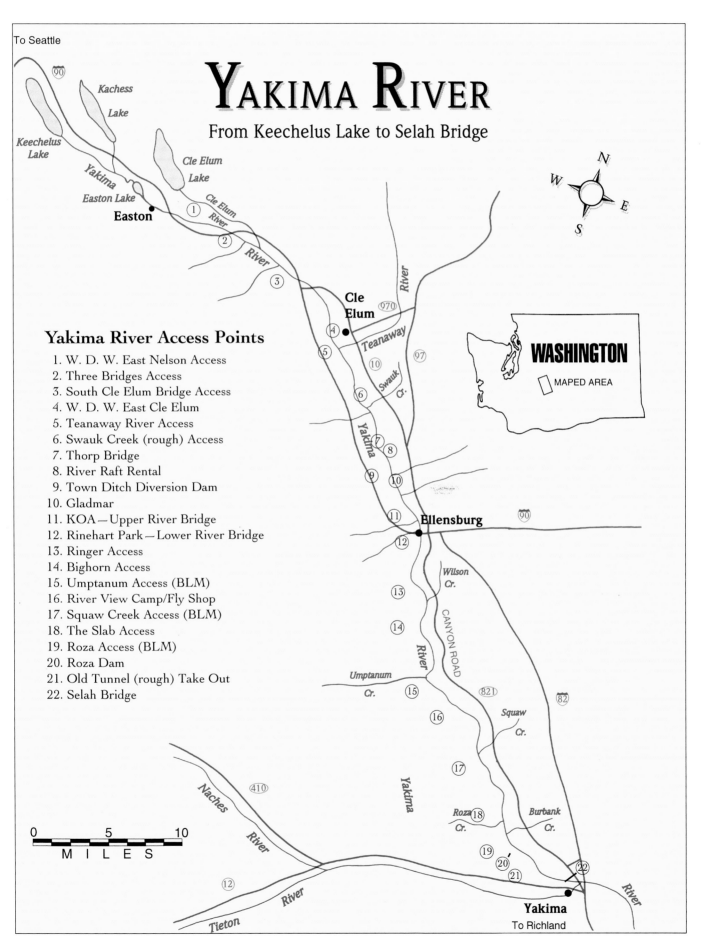

YAKIMA RIVER
From Keechelus Lake to Selah Bridge

To Seattle

Kachess Lake

Keechelus Lake

Cle Elum Lake

Easton Lake

Easton

WASHINGTON
MAPED AREA

Yakima River Access Points

1. W. D. W. East Nelson Access
2. Three Bridges Access
3. South Cle Elum Bridge Access
4. W. D. W. East Cle Elum
5. Teanaway River Access
6. Swauk Creek (rough) Access
7. Thorp Bridge
8. River Raft Rental
9. Town Ditch Diversion Dam
10. Gladmar
11. KOA—Upper River Bridge
12. Rinehart Park—Lower River Bridge
13. Ringer Access
14. Bighorn Access
15. Umptanum Access (BLM)
16. River View Camp/Fly Shop
17. Squaw Creek Access (BLM)
18. The Slab Access
19. Roza Access (BLM)
20. Roza Dam
21. Old Tunnel (rough) Take Out
22. Selah Bridge

Cle Elum

Teanaway

Swauk Cr.

Yakima

Ellensburg

Wilson Cr.

CANYON ROAD

River

Umptanum Cr.

Squaw Cr.

Burbank Cr.

Roza Cr.

Yakima

Naches River

Tieton River

Yakima
To Richland

MILES
0   5   10

Cecil Probasco with a Yakima River rainbow taken in the upper river near Cle Elum.

YAKIMA RIVER

◆

THROUGH MY TEN-YEAR-OLD EYES THE YAKIMA was a monstrous river. I was not allowed to fish there—it was much too dangerous, with currents too strong for a skinny, tennis-shoed kid to wade. My dad once told me a scare story about a girl and a horse swallowed and drowned by a gigantic whirlpool. Maybe it was true . . . maybe it wasn't. But I was told to never go down to the river by myself. And I didn't.

Instead, I would spend my summer days walking the banks of a small meadow stream that ran through my uncle's ranch. Countless afternoons passed while I lackadaisically walked the stream, drifting worms and grasshoppers to eager rainbows. Most were under ten inches in length, but it didn't matter, it was all I knew of fishing and the fishing was great. I loved it. I lived for it. It was on this stream that I learned to fish. It was on this stream that I learned patience and a lot about life.

Eventually, within two or three miles from my uncle's house, the stream cascaded down a steep embankment into a channel of the Yakima River. A few times, and only with my dad or uncle along, I was allowed to walk down to the high bank overlooking the Yakima. My eyes would widen and body tense as I stared, overwhelmed by the enormity of the river. I felt scared just standing there on the bluff but, even so, I longed to fish in the big river. If I could catch a bunch of little fish in the stream I could surely catch many bigger ones in the Yakima.

Once, when my cousin visited from Colorado he went down to the river while I fished the stream. He was also told not to go near the river but went anyway. He tried to talk me into going, but I didn't want to get into trouble and, besides, that big whirlpool and the girl and horse were still fixed in my mind. I fished as close to the embankment where the stream entered the river as I dared that day, farther than I ever had before. I even put my rod down and sneaked up to the high bank hoping to catch a glimpse of my cousin fishing in the river. He was nowhere to be seen so I hurried back to the stream and my rod before I got caught. When my cousin returned he had a stringer full of fish larger than I had ever seen.

From that day on the Yakima was on my mind a good deal of the time. Oh, how I wanted to catch a stringer of fish like my cousin. It was several years before it happened, and when that long anticipated event finally came, my bait rod had been replaced by a fly rod and I was tying my own crude flies.

I remember my first trip to the river like my first date—it was just about as awkward too. I did manage to catch a fish on my hand-tied Carey Special and I was as proud as could be. This was the largest trout of my life thus far and I couldn't wait to get home with the 14-inch rainbow to show my dad. I had become a fly fisherman.

A lot has happened in my life since those first summers spent fishing for trout in the little meadow stream and later the Yakima River. And even though I now travel to famous streams and rivers beyond my wildest dreams when I was a kid, my mind always drifts back to my home water—the Yakima. Now I fish it as often as time allows. Although my techniques, tackle and the fishery itself have improved considerably since those pioneering days, it is those early days when my love affair with the river began that I remember and cherish most.

History

WHEN CONGRESS DIRECTED THE WAR DEPARTMENT to make preliminary surveys for a rail system linking the Pacific Coast with the Mississippi Valley in 1853, President Franklin Pierce assigned Isaac I. Stevens, who had recently been appointed Governor of Washington Territory, to explore the northern regions. Stevens appointed George B. McClellan to explore a route through the Cascade Mountains.

The route taken by McClellan followed the Yakima River throughout it's course, from Fort Walla Walla to the lakes just below the present Snoqualmie Pass. Although McClellan was not the first white explorer to visit this area he was the first to spend any amount of time there. Previous white visitors came mostly in search of furs and horses of which they found many especially in the Kittitas Valley.

In all probability McClellan was the first white man to ever fish the Yakima River and with certainty he was the first to fly fish it. In a passage taken from The Journal of George B. McClellan, May 20, 1853 - December 15, 1853, McClellan made this entry on Sunday, Sept. 4, 1853. "Camp No. 30. Yakima River. High wind directly in our faces all day long. After getting into camp, fished up the stream about 3/4m unsuccessfully with salmon fly & the brown & black hackles—not a rise."

Was McClellan using a salmon fly of the Atlantic genre? Or was he using a floating fly; a salmon fly, a stonefly? There is a hatch of stoneflies in early September on the Yakima; in the passage when McClellan states "not a rise" did he fail to actually bring a fish to the surface with a tempting adult stonefly pattern?

A later passage keeps this question stirring in me. After following the river all the way to the divide now known as Snoqualmie Pass, McClellan talks of "Lake Kah-chess" and the entry reads: "Went down to the lake in the P.M., tried fishing but the wretches would not rise to the fly." Could "would not rise to the fly" mean a dry fly?

It is interesting to note that McClellan makes reference several times to the prolific runs of salmon in the Yakima River, (called 'Yakinse' by the time McClellan's party reached the Kittitas Valley) runs that today are nearly non-existent. McClellan makes reference to Lake "Kitchelas" which he says is the head of the "Yakinse." He also mentions Lake "Kah-chess" and a passage in his journal reads: "The first dam we passed this morning is formed by setting up at intervals across the stream tripods of timber, about 20 feet high, one big one downstream & the other two in the direction of the dam—legs are tied from one frame to the next, & vertical ones (with the slope of plane of the two upper legs of the tripod) lashed to these. A wickerwork laid against these closed the passage to the fish; & from stands below this the salmon are speared by men standing ready for them."

◆

Irrigation of farmland in Yakima Canyon.

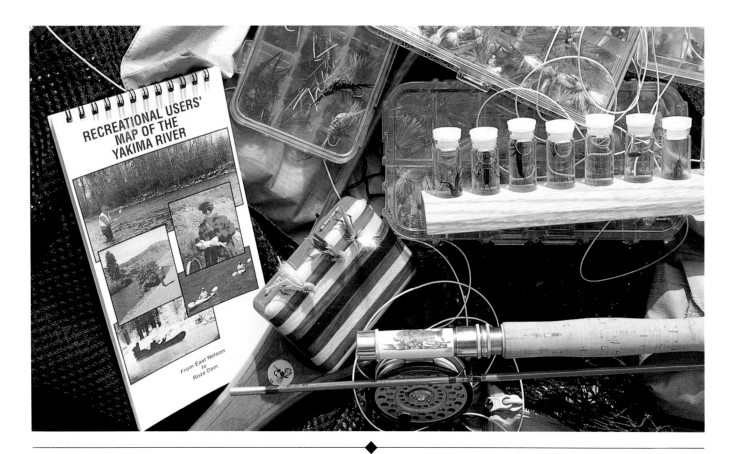

After McClellan's exploratory trip along the Yakima the fur trade increased along the river system. Besides trappers, horse and cattle ranchers and farmers began to settle. The Kittitas Valley, in the central portion of the Yakima River, attracted a large number of homesteaders when the U.S. Government opened the valley to homesteading in 1867. Gold was discovered in the Wenatchee Mountains in the 1860s and 1870s which also brought a flood of people into the area. The Yakima River and the valleys through which it flowed were in for a change.

Parts of eastern Washington are officially classified as desert with an average annual rainfall of less than 10 inches. The area from Ellensburg through the Yakima Canyon to the south is included in this climatic heading. With the coming of the farmer came the need for irrigation. The logical source for water in the Yakima and Kittitas Valleys of course was the Yakima River. Reservoirs were built near Snoqualmie Pass on lakes Kachess, Keechelus, Easton and Cle Elum to store and regulate the flow of water in the upper Yakima River. Lake Kachess was first, built in 1912. Lake Cle Elum was largest and last, constructed in 1933. Roza Dam (1939) in the Yakima Canyon, Bumping Lake, Clear Lake (1914) and Rimrock Lake (1925) near White Pass, were built to control the flow in the lower valley. Diversions dams and canals were built to bring life to the fertile valleys.

Little regard was given to the anadromous fish of the river system and with the building of Sunnyside Diversion Dam in 1891 (the first on the river) steelhead and salmon in the upper Yakima began a downward spiral that would ultimately bring them close to extinction. It wasn't until 1929 that Sunnyside Diversion Dam was laddered and by this time the damage had been done. In addition with the building of Roza Dam, although a ladder was built at the time of construction, passage was difficult for fish during low water periods before stringent regulations concerning water flow were adopted and enforced.

In recent history the Yakima River has undergone many changes. Although the salmon and steelhead (except for a struggling few) are gone, wise management has created an exceptional trout fishery in the upper and central river valleys from Easton Dam through the Yakima Canyon and beyond.

During the 1980s the Yakima's management included many positive regulation changes. In 1983 a Selective Fishery Designation was placed on the river from the mouth of Wilson Creek to the mouth of the Teanaway River with limited creel, gear and size restrictions. Also in 1983 the Game Department stopped planting the river with hatchery trout in favor of natural propagation. In 1986 bait was prohibited from Roza to Easton. Then in 1988 the entire portion of prime trout water on the Yakima River from Roza to Easton was placed under Selective Fishery status, with single-barbless-hooks required. In 1990 the Yakima River became a catch-and-release fishery from Roza to Easton and in 1991 was opened to year-round fishing in this section. Average trout sizes began to increase. The quality of fishing began to improve. Today the Yakima River is an outstanding blue ribbon fishery in every sense of the term.

The River

*D*URING THE SUMMER MONTHS THE YAKIMA RIVER begins it's journey as a rolling, tumbling torrent, not like most mountain streams which begin as a collection of snow melt trickles uniting as small rivulets and streams merging to form larger streams, collecting with yet others to eventually form a river in a romantic kind of way. Near Snoqualmie Pass at an elevation of nearly 3,000 feet, the Yakima shoots through pipes beneath Keechelus Dam right in the heart of the Cascade Mountains and immediately becomes a river.

Of course the river is joined along the way by numerous mountain streams and continually gains flow. Some streams are significant drainages in their own right. Rivers like the Cle Elum and Teanaway, which drain a large part of this mountainous area, empty into the upper Yakima as it makes its way to the valleys below. By the time the river reaches Kittitas Valley it has traveled roughly 50 miles and has been joined by numerous smaller streams. But the Yakima is not wild and out of control and seldom is even during spring runoff because it's major source (snowmelt) is carefully controlled by reservoirs and dams. This wasn't always the case.

Snowpack in the headwaters is significant. In the past there have been times when after a particularly heavy snow season followed by a late, wet spring the river has flooded. Probably the worst flood on record is known as the Vanport Flood, named after the Portland-area town along the Columbia River which was completely destroyed. The event took place on Memorial Day weekend in 1948. All tributaries of the Columbia River were at flood stage due to heavy rains and large snowpack in the Cascades. The Yakima River was measured at the Sunnyside Diversion Dam with flows reaching 37,700 cfs. To put that figure in perspective, during summer months when the river is running at it's highest, the average flow is just over 4,000 cfs.

After the "big flood" plans to avert such disasters in the future were developed. A flood forecast was designed for the Columbia River and all it's tributaries and careful flood control operations began.

During summer months the Kittitas Valley appears from a distance as an oasis, a Shangrila of green surrounded by the tawny summer grasses of this arid land. All thanks to the river. The fertile valley is renowned for it's alfalfa hay crop and beef cattle industry.

When the Yakima leaves the Kittitas Valley it flows through a picturesque canyon, winding snake-like through sage

The Tieton River just below Rimrock Lake, a popular river for whitewater rafting during the high discharges of fall.

Keechelus Lake to Cle Elum

*Y*OU ARE TRESSPASSING ON BUREAU OF RECLA-
mation land if you walk into the base of Keechelus Dam,
the starting point of the Yakima River. Once I did just so I could
see the beginning of the stream. I wish I hadn't made the trip.
The river shoots through a concrete tunnel near the bottom of
the reservoir, down a fenced, cement canal. It's an ugly start to
a beautiful trout stream.

Just a couple of miles downstream the river passes by
Crystal Springs campground operated by the U.S. Forest
Service. During high water months of summer the river is a torrent here, an unmerciful flow created for distant farmlands.
With banks brimming it rushes through log jams and sweepers
and it's a very dangerous section of river. This area receives little angling attention during the high flow period for obvious
reasons.

By mid-September when the irrigation flows of the Yakima
have ended this upper section takes on a whole new look. The
once raging river is but a trickle by comparison. The power and
fury of the summer stream is obvious while walking the river
channel. Log jams high and dry, gouges carved deep in the river
floor and newly deposited river rock depict the water's force.

Fishing the upper reaches of the Yakima this time of year
is similar to many mountain streams. Trout tend to be on the
smallish size but often come easily to any dry fly passed their
way. Most trout are rainbows but the occasional cutthroat or
brook trout will be landed also.

*The start of the Yakima River at the base of Keechelus Dam
during the low water flows of fall.*

◆

Warning sign to the hazards of manipulated water flow of the Yakima River.

and grass covered hills and eventually to the city of Yakima,
some 30 miles distant. It is joined by a few small streams along
this section, but none significantly add to the flow. What is significant about this section is the trout fishery. Many feel it is
the best the river has to offer. I will talk about this in more
detail later on.

Just before the river reaches Yakima it breaks out of the
canyon and is joined by the Naches River, another major tributary. From that junction on as the river makes it's way
through the lower valley it takes on a completely different look.
The river widens and slows, nourishing orchards, vineyards
and vast expanses of produce throughout the lower valley.

By this point in the Yakima's journey it has warmed to
where trout no longer flourish and all resemblances to a trout
stream have disappeared. The Yakima is eventually joined by
several more creeks and canals in the lower valley and the pace
continually slows to it's confluence with the Columbia River at
the city of Richland. The total distance the river covers from
start to finish is about 215 miles, with roughly 75 miles being
prime trout water.

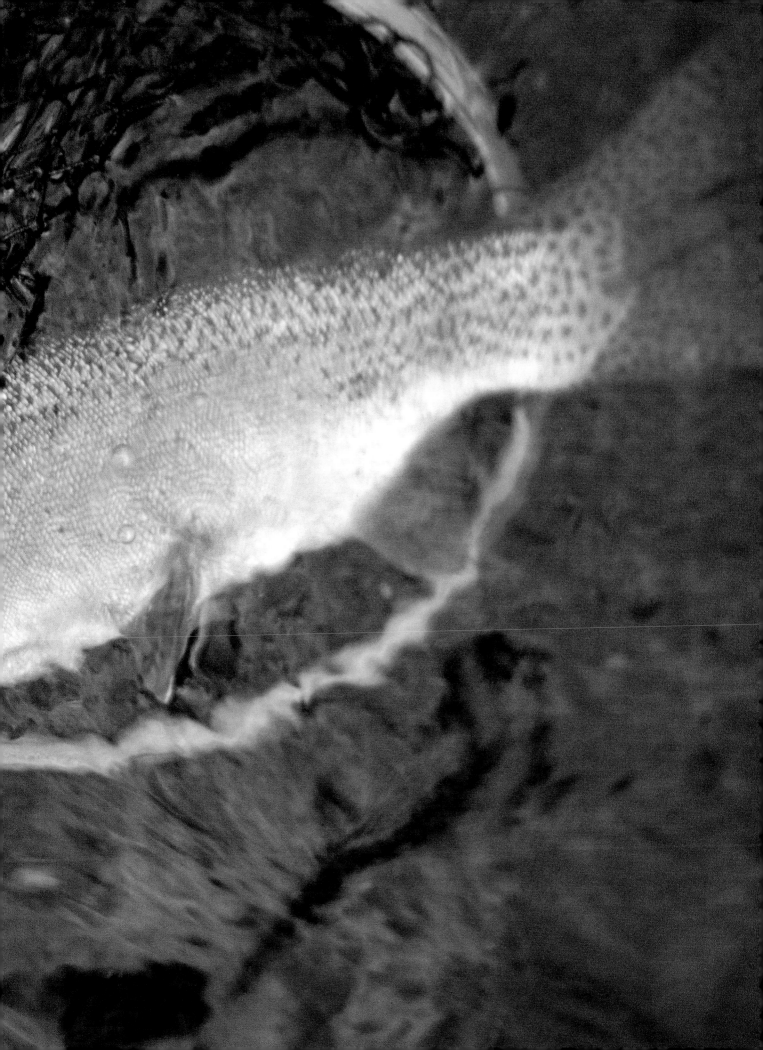

It is a pleasure to walk and fish the river here but this is not the Yakima that gained blue ribbon fame; that Yakima appears farther downstream. Still, there is nothing quite like a fall afternoon walking down a small mountain stream casting dry flies into every small pocket or pool. And what must the resident trout think after surviving the mayhem of their summer struggle in the savage currents only to sip insects from the peaceful flow of fall?

After about 10 miles of flow the river comes to another reservoir, Lake Easton. Here irrigation water is diverted into the large Main Canal by Easton Diversion Dam and ultimately provides water to Kittitas Valley. The terrain mellows from this point on, but there are still log jams and large sweepers making it too hazardous to drift.

Much of the river in this area runs through private land and public access is poor. All my life I have heard stories from old-timers about the trout fishing around Easton. I have only fished in this area a couple of times and didn't catch anything to write home about on either occasion. But still those stories are intriguing. Becoming best friends with a land owner in the Easton area might be a good idea.

From 400 feet below the Easton Dam to Roza Dam, nearly 70 miles distant, the Yakima River's Catch-and-Release regulations are in effect. Fishing is open year-round and is limited to flies or lures with single, barbless hooks.

The Washington Department of Wildlife developed a launch site just west of the East Nelson Siding of Interstate 90. This is the highest boat launch on the river and the first public access point. Still, it is not recommended for floating except by experienced boaters in easily maneuverable and stoppable craft. Log jams, sharp corners and sweepers are a hazard that must be dealt with in this section.

A few miles downstream there is another access point known as Three Bridges. The same types of water will be found all the way down to the mouth of the Cle Elum River and the aforementioned obstacles will be encountered. There is another rough access point at South Cle Elum Bridge.

When the river enters the valley of the Cle Elum it broadens and gains even more strength from this river that drains a large portion of the alpine regions of central Washington. And although the river drains such a vast area, runoff is not a problem here either since the Cle Elum River flows through yet another reservoir, Lake Cle Elum, the drainage system's largest. From the lake it is only a few short miles to the river's confluence with the Yakima.

The only problem with runoff in the upper stretches of the Yakima comes from poor logging practices, i.e, clear-cutting. One early May morning I traveled to the Yakima for a few days of fishing with a friend. The weather had become unseasonably warm across the state the previous day. There was still a healthy snowpack in the mountains but the reservoirs protect the river from surges of snow melt. When we arrived at the river it was flowing chocolate brown. My friend, coming all the way from Wyoming to fish with me during this prime time on the Yakima was a bit disgruntled, observing the river to be "too thick to drink, and too thin to plow."

Many anglers, local businesses, guides, etc., were effected by the runoff which lasted for over a week. A concerned friend who makes his living on the river traced the chocolate flow back to it's source. You guessed it, a couple of feeder streams below the reservoirs, that just happened to be located in clear-cut areas! When will we learn? Or will we, as long as there is a dollar to be made?

Fishing the river in the Cle Elum area is very popular. Wading fishermen have no problem finding a spot on the water and although the gentle flows of fall make for easier wading, this area is also good for the boatless angler during higher flows of summer. There is a dike road with public access on the south side of town and good river access to the east of town. For the floating fisherman, there is a Department of Wildlife Access area in East Cle Elum, near the intersection of Highway 10 and Highway 970, the link to Swauk Pass.

The river in this area is generally clear, cold and flows over a mostly rocky bottom. To view the river here one would never guess it's beginning. It is this part of the river where the majority of remaining salmon stocks return to spawn. Walking the stream in late fall will reveal salmon redds marked on streamside foliage with colored flags. Native Americans have been keeping track of returning fish and it is their goal to bring the once tremendous run of anadromous fish back to the river.

Although not the most generous section on the river for size of trout, the Cle Elum area produces some very nice fish. I have one angling friend who boasts of a 22-inch rainbow taken near town, a commendable trout in any section of the river.

Hatches on the Yakima are fairly reliable and consistent (see Flies, Gear, Hatches). The river in the Cle Elum area will experience respective hatches at nearly the same time as lower sections of the river with slight variances from year-to-year. However, this area hosts a hatch of October caddis in the fall and even though sporadic they are much more plentiful than on lower sections of the river.

If luck be with you and you happen to be on the water during a hatch of October caddis, fishing can be a circus—a feeding frenzy of feeding frenzies! A size 8, orange Stimulator is your ticket to ecstasy for catching a stake of rainbow trout on big dry flies

Careless logging destruction of the watershed near Snoqualmie Pass.

The upper Yakima River near the town of Cle Elum.

Upper River: Cle Elum to Ellensburg

A YOUNG BUCK DEER STANDS DRINKING FROM the Yakima's clear cool water on a brisk October morning. Steam shoots from his nostrils as he spots your boat and then dashes off into the security of the giant cottonwoods, the leaves now brilliantly yellowed as winter quickly approaches. A bald eagle sits in a treetop as you round the next turn, oblivious to your presence. Around each corner there is some other awe-inspiring form of nature. And the trout. Oh yes, we can't forget the trout. The upper river is a special place in the fall.

For reference when I mention the upper river I am talking in fishing jargon placing myself in Ellensburg, in the heart of this blue ribbon stream. Locally upper river means the river above Ellensburg. The lower river is the section of river from Ellensburg downstream through the canyon.

The Yakima is a river of many faces. Throughout it's journey the Yakima transforms as it passes through several climatic and geological regions.

When not running wild with unnatural summer flows, from it's source to Cle Elum it presents itself first as a mountain stream, and then becomes a mountain river as it is joined by tributaries along the way. When the river reaches Cle Elum it widens and slows and is joined by another major tributary, the Teanaway River. During spring and summer flows rafters usually enter the Teanaway at the point where it is crossed by Highway 10, a few miles east of Cle Elum, and float the short distance to it's confluence with the Yakima.

Highway 10 was the main road between Ellensburg and Seattle before Interstate 90 was built. At a point not too far from the Teanaway, the Yakima enters a canyon and winds through the hills for several miles. Highway 10 parallels the river throughout the canyon and offers plenty of access to bank and wading fishermen.

As the river makes it's way eastward through the canyon the rain-shadow effect of the Cascade Mountains becomes strikingly obvious. The fir and cedar trees of the mountains have given way to pines and other dry-land vegetation. And when traveling across the mountains from the coast you usually run out of bad weather, be it rain or snow, by the time you are halfway between Ellensburg and Cle Elum. Usually replacing the moisture though, are the incessant winds of the Kittitas Valley which certainly make the careful presentation of a tiny dry fly interesting.

The upper river, from either the Department of Wildlife's Access Area in East Cle Elum, from the Teanaway River, or from a rough launch where Swauk Creek enters the Yakima, down to one of the distant access points, is a very popular stretch of the Yakima for rafting and drift boat fishermen and there are few obstacles along the way. One point of caution: A couple of miles past the Teanaway River's confluence with the

Yakima, and just past the power line crossing, a wasteway flume sometimes discharges into the river creating a hazard on the right bank. It's best to hug the left bank of the river after passing under the power lines . . . just in case!

During summer flows the river is moving swiftly and boaters can make good time floating through the canyon. However, this section of river can be incredibly slow during fall conditions, especially when there is wind blowing upstream. Do not try a longer float than you can complete during the short days of autumn or you may be caught on the river when the sun disappears with your car nowhere in sight. I know from experience.

There is an abandoned railroad grade that snakes along the river, and the shore-bound fisherman can easily walk along viewing the river and choosing the water he wishes to fish. The largest trout I hooked in the Yakima (and I want to emphasize the word 'hooked') came while I walked this railroad grade and fished among the boulders at the water's edge. It was a tremendous rainbow, beyond doubt the largest trout I have ever seen in the Yakima. But as many large fish do this one made me pay the price and after a fierce battle that I almost won a couple of times, it broke me off in the rocks.

Besides normal hatches and dry fly fishing which I will cover in more detail later, I have found stretches in the upper river (like the one just described) to be particularly good for working large streamers. Every turn of the river that comes near the old railroad grade has large boulders that were placed to prevent a washout of the tracks. These areas remain deep

Steve Probasco fishing the Yakima during the fall near the town of Cle Elum.

Geese along the upper river are a common sight during the fall.

◆

and create superb shelter and feeding stations.

I have found the fish in such places to be a bit larger than in other parts of the river and flies such as Muddlers, Spuddlers, Matukas and Woolley Buggers have been the patterns most productive for me. Using heavy, sink-tip lines so that streamers swim and dart among the rocks is the best way to fish them. Oh, and use a heavy tippet of 1X or 2X to avoid losing the largest fish in the river to the rocks . . . like someone I know!

Eventually the river exits the canyon and twists away from the highway. For a few miles the river is accessible to only the floating fisherman as it winds through more farmland and eventually crosses under Thorp Bridge. Launching or taking a boat out here is difficult and the usual choice is to continue floating the four miles down to the diversion dam. Highway 10 again parallels the river from the bridge to the dam, and there are several access points for the wading fisherman.

Boaters must exit the river before the diversion dam. About a mile before the dam there is a take-out on property owned by River Raft Rentals. A small fee is charged for the use of the ramp which is located on the left side of the river. Rafters can also take-out just before the dam, again, on the left bank.

There is one more floatable stretch of river before reaching Ellensburg, this being the float from Gladmar Park to the Upper River Bridge and KOA campground near the I-90 Interchange, just west of town. Gladmar Park is located right behind the big fruit stand seen from Interstate 90, at exit 101.

The nearly five mile float down to the KOA campground parallels I-90 the entire distance. This is a fairly straight stretch of water that is easy to float and is a good choice for those on a

limited time schedule. There is plenty of quality water along the way and you can stretch this section out over several hours, or row down to the KOA in a jiffy.

As you approach the bridge you will see the old Ellensburg Power House along the right bank of the river. The take-out is just above the bridge on the left bank. A permit to park and take-out here can be obtained in the KOA office.

During my teen years while living in Ellensburg I would often fish the section of river that now parallels the freeway just west of town. I would start out fishing Reecer Creek or Dry Creek at the point where they cross under Highway 10 and follow them down to the river.

Back in those days (1960s) these two creeks were both great trout streams, as were most of the creeks that enter the river in the Kittitas Valley. At their confluence with the Yakima River the fishing was dynamite.

It was at the mouth of Reecer Creek where I caught my largest brookie. It was the largest trout of any type that I had heard of anyone catching in the Yakima. The fish had to have weighed four pounds or better.

Brook trout are rare in the Yakima now but electrofishing has shown there to be a few small ones still around. The majority of the fish in the Cle Elum to Ellensburg section are rainbows, with the odd brookie, cutthroat or bull trout sometimes hooked.

◆

An old irrigation flume that has since been replaced by pumping stations.

Ellensburg to the Mouth of

Yakima Canyon

*F*ROM THE KOA CAMPGROUND DOWNSTREAM TO THE Lower River Bridge floaters should be aware of narrow channels and sweepers. For this reason, most fishermen take-out at the KOA.

However, this two mile section of river between the Upper River Bridge and the Lower River Bridge is accessible and a productive stretch for the walking/wading fisherman. The best approach is from Rinehart Park, located near the Lower River Bridge. A good trail follows the river upstream providing access to the water.

This area doesn't get a lot of pressure; most anglers head to the more popular and floatable stretches of the river. There are side channels and deep slots and pools that deserve attention here, the serious fly fisherman can do quite well. It is a good spot to fish if you are limited in time.

The perfect match to the October Caddis,— an Orange Stimulator.

◆

Ray Pelland releasing a Yakima Canyon rainbow.

The Yakima hosts a sizable number of Rocky Mountain whitefish and during winter months whitefish anglers come out in force. This area, due to the pools and long tailouts, is a popular destination for whitefish anglers. Although fishing on this section of river falls within the catch-and-release, selective fishery regulations, when fishing for whitefish there is an exception. Bait and a single-pointed, barbed hook may be used for whitefish only, from December 1 through the last day of February.

There are three small streams that spill into the Yakima along the west bank of the river in this section between the two bridges. The meadow stream I reminisced about at the start of this book empties into the river here. Fishing the mouths of these streams is generally productive and can produce some remarkable fish. During the high flow of summer the mouths of the little streams and much of the good water will be unreachable to the wading angler, but after the water drops in the fall the whole area can be easily waded.

The section of river between Lower River Bridge and the mouth of Yakima Canyon is not advisable to float. This area is heavily braided with channels and is full of sweepers and downed trees. It can be floated though and I have done it. However, I won't do it again. There are easier and safer floats on the river where the fishing is just as good.

Below the Lower River Bridge and Rinehart Park the Yakima flows through farmland and there is little public access. Since this is a dangerous stretch to float it gets little fishing pressure. This is a five mile stretch of river that should be attempted by only the most experienced of rafters with paid-up life insurance.

The first safe access point for boaters below the Lower River Bridge is the Washington Department of Wildlife's concrete launch known as the Ringer Road Access Area located just before the entrance to the Yakima Canyon.

Wading fishermen in the Yakima Canyon during the early fall.

Lower River: Yakima Canyon

Cactus found in the thirsty hills of the Yakima Canyon.

Cactus found in the thirsty hills of the Yakima Canyon.

*F*ROM THE RINGER ACCESS AREA THE RIVER TRAVELS less than one mile before entering the majestic Yakima Canyon. Immediately it is joined by Wilson Creek, a significant tributary, at the mouth of the canyon. Wilson Creek runs brown with irrigation runoff during summer and it's effects are noticeable in the river from this point on. The river, although not dirty, is not sparkling clean either.

Many fishermen feel that the section of river that flows through the Yakima Canyon is best. For roughly 20 miles the Yakima winds through the arid canyon, parallelled the entire distance by Highway 821. Access for bank and wading anglers is good and the entire section is a float fisherman's paradise. Nearly every foot of the river screams TROUT!

Much of central Washington sits upon the great Columbia River Plateau, one of the largest volcanic flood basalts in the world. Through fissures extremely fluid magma suddenly spurted to the surface of the earth spreading out across a vast area. Over the millennia such events covered much of the Pacific Northwest.

The Yakima Canyon is testimony to the awesome forces of nature and time. The layers of basalt visible in canyon walls are part of this flood basalt which is estimated to be over 10,000 feet thick in places.

In only 70 miles of travel the Yakima has flowed from a

Looking north through the mouth of Yakima Canyon towards Mount Stuart and the Stuart Range.

A beautiful Yakima Canyon rainbow.

watershed with an annual rainfall of 80 inches to a desert setting of less than 10 inches of moisture. The tawny colored grasses and sage that cover the hills of the canyon, the cactus found along the banks of the river, and critters like small scorpions found under rocks and rattlesnakes, are all testimony to this thirsty land.

Wildlife abounds in the canyon. A variety of birds and game can be seen along the river and hills above. Raptors and water-fowl fill the air while deer and bighorn sheep make regular appearances to the delight of those who frequent the canyon. The bighorn sheep population originated from the planting of a dozen sheep from the Penticton area of British Columbia in 1971. It is now estimated that there are over 150 sheep in this herd which are easily viewed from Highway 821 during fall and winter months while they wander the hills of the canyon.

The Yakima River Canyon is, in simple terms, dry fly heav-en. Dependable hatches can be found eight months of the year, starting in March and continuing through October (see the sec-tion on hatches). Even during winter months trout frequently rise to midges each afternoon and the patient angler can try his luck during the brief hatches of these tiny insects, providing the river isn't frozen over, but that only happens for brief periods during particularly hard winters.

Electrofishing done in the canyon reveals that the trout are mostly rainbows with a few cutthroat mixed in. In the 1960s brown trout were planted in the canyon but didn't take. Once in a while there is a report of someone catching a brown, but I have never talked to anyone who has personally caught one.

During the course of an average day of floating through the canyon a good angler can expect to catch fish ranging from 10 to 18 inches and depending on skill, the possibilities of a fish 20 inches or better certainly exist.

A private trout study in the canyon revealed at least five dis-tinct races of rainbows—fish that were introduced from distant locations. The river has not been planted since 1983, and now all rainbows found in the Yakima are a genetic mixture of wild and hatchery trout but are considered wild because they spawn naturally.

Even if you don't hook one of the 20 inchers found in the Yakima you will usually see them feeding tight against the banks. You will often witness a big guy raise to your fly and refuse it at the last moment. This usually means there was something not quite right with your fly, the drift, or maybe your tippet spooked it. These fish didn't get big by being careless and catching the largest trout can be as demanding as in any other technical river.

Since catch-and-release regulations came into effect in 1990 the number of large four and five-year-olds (20+ inches) has risen. However, they are increasingly harder to catch. With the increase in pressure on the river more exact imitations of natur-al insects and precise, delicate presentation are required for larg-er fish.

During high water months the most productive way to fish the canyon is to drift at current speed casting a short line to within a couple of inches of overhanging grasses, branches and other streamside foliage. One inch is even better and five inches is too far from the action. Big fish simply won't leave their feeding station to take a fly or even a natural. If you can't keep your fly floating drag free, in tight against the bank, you simply won't catch fish save for the occasional small one.

One of the easiest times on the Yakima, when trout seem to lose some of their caution, is during mid-summer when the hoppers are out. Trout sometimes slam hopper patterns with reckless abandon and they will often chase this larger morsel a little farther than they would a smaller insect. You can get by with a larger tippet, your fly is easier to see on the water and the fishing is less demanding.

There is one other insect that will create a frenzy and send the trout in a tail-spin. And that is a stonefly hatch of which there are several on this river. Trout will appear out of nowhere for a drifting Stimulator, in the appropriate color, when they are tuned into the adults.

Over the course of the day a serious fisherman will make several hundred casts during a summer float, repeatedly casting flies near the bank. This is very focused fishing with little room for error. It is reasonable though for a good caster to raise 30 to 50 fish on a float down the canyon. And if luck be with you a few of those will be in the 18 to 20 inch range.

There are several good boat launch sites in the canyon. The first is the Bighorn launch area which is the starting point for many canyon floaters. When the water is high you can cover a great distance in the course of a day. Most floaters like to start at Bighorn, or even back at Ringers for a full day's float. Fishing is

A guided trip in the Yakima Canyon during the high water flows of summer.

Bighorn sheep are often seen roaming the hills of the canyon. They can sometimes be spotted along, or in the river like this ram.

good from the moment you start. As I mentioned fish the banks with an appropriate dry fly and pay particular attention to areas with overhanging structure providing shade.

Six miles downstream you will come to a cable suspension bridge crossing the river. Just past the bridge is the Umptanum Recreation Area maintained by the Bureau of Land Management. This is a good launch spot for short floats or exit for fishermen who started farther upstream.

Crossing the bridge and walking up Umptanum Creek Valley is a good way to view up close the flora and fauna of this spectacular region. The creek eventually takes you after several miles to a beautiful waterfall back in the hills. If you make the journey be aware that this is rattlesnake country.

From the Umptanum launch, after following the river for a couple of miles, you will come to a private launch on the left shore belonging to River View Resort owned by Red and Marlene Blankenship. This little resort offers R.V. and tent camping, vehicle shuttle, well equipped fishing raft rentals and a last minute fly shop featuring all of the Yakima's hottest patterns.

It is two and one-half miles from River View Resort to the next BLM Access Area at Squaw Creek. The same types of water will be found in this stretch as in previous stretches throughout the canyon. A point to note: wading fishermen find these public access areas along the canyon to be good starting points for their efforts. Great fishing can be had at all of them.

Three more miles of river will land you at a launch/take-out area known as The Slab. Many years ago there were buildings on this site and the concrete slabs remain. Most fishermen have exited the river before or at The Slab. If you continue downstream, you will pass Roza Creek on your right, and a mile or so farther, Burbank Creek on your left and then you will come to the final pullout at the Roza Access Area where all floaters must exit. Roza Dam is just around the corner!

Fishing is not the only recreation to be found in the Yakima Canyon. From the Roza Access Area to the dam water skiing and jet-skis are popular on hot summer days. In April of 1993 the Kittitas County Board of Commissioners passed an ordinance prohibiting all motorized watercraft from the Roza Access Area upstream to the railroad trestle near the mouth of the canyon. This was a definite bonus for fishermen.

Ellensburg is a college town and hot summer weather creates an inner-tube hatch in the canyon. Every imaginable floating craft appears on the river operated by every imaginable type operator. This is not usually a problem for the fisherman though, as the floaters mostly stay in the middle of the river away from the fishing action.

Paragliding is also a growing sport in the canyon. The hills and weather in the canyon provide optimum conditions. Just past the Umptanum Access Area, along a ridge on the left wall of the canyon, wind-socks can be seen towering above the crest. Paragliding is taught here and on most weekends throughout summer and fall, gliders can be seen working the air currents high above the river.

The highway speed limit in the canyon is 45 mph. From May 15 to September 15 there is a ban on all truck traffic on the canyon road, but come September 15 the trucks come roaring back creating a hazard for all recreational users. It is my opinion that truck traffic should be banned from the canyon.

When fall approaches and irrigation of Kittitas Valley has ended for the season the lower river, just like the upper river, becomes a completely different stream. The flow drops below 2,000 cfs and you can wade the river almost anywhere you choose. For many fall is the zenith in the Yakima Canyon.

By fall even fish that weren't so difficult at the beginning of the season can now be hair-pulling obstinate. The main entree in the trout's top water diet will be the tiny *Baetis* mayfly which will appear each afternoon for a spell when the water warms. Fishermen who can deliver a delicate line and are good with presentation will catch fish. Those who can't . . . well, let's just say I have seen quite a few disappointed fishermen on the river during fall.

By late October dry fly action winds down. The nights get frosty and I change my tactics from working the *Baetis* beds to

A bright Yakima Canyon rainbow taken on a small dry fly.

Stonefly cases found on the rocks is a common sight along the Yakima River.

◆

fishing some of the deeper pools and runs with streamers. I switch from floating lines to a heavy Teeny 200, sinking-tip line, equipped with a big sculpin imitation. Some of my largest fish of the season succumb to this tactic each fall and I will keep this up until my fingers and brain are numbed from the cold.

Roza Dam to Selah

*J*UST BEFORE ROZA DAM, HEADING SOUTH ON HIGHWAY 821, the highway climbs sharply up a hill with a hairpin turn at the top. There is a frightening cliff on the right that drops down to the river in the deep gorge below. Immediately below the dam, the river rounds it's first turn and quiets into a large pool below the cliffs. Access is from a trail that leaves the parking area at the top of the hill. It is a steep walk down to the river.

Without a boat you are very limited in the amount of fishable water in this stretch of river. In fact you can't even cover the first pool effectively. You can walk the old railroad grade that runs along the river but even then you will end up walking quite a distance to fish water that gets pounded mostly by bait fishermen. The selective fishery regulations are not in effect below Roza Dam.

Still, there is good fishing to be found below the dam if you can get to the far side of the river. This means packing some type of soft boat down the hill. Most boats are too heavy and impractical to pack to the bottom of the gorge. My Tote 'N Float is perfect for such a task.

The biggest problem with taking a boat downstream from

here is that there are not any good spots to exit the river. The best location I have found is downstream approximately three miles at the point where Highway 821 comes closest to the river. It is easily viewed when driving down the hill from above the dam. There is also an old tunnel boring through the hillside which the canyon road used to go through. Even here you have to climb and carry your boat up a short rock bank, across the railroad tracks, down a bank, and back up another to get to your car. But if you go past this point the next spot to take out is at Selah Bridge a few miles farther downstream. The old tunnel exit is definitely best.

The big pool below the dam had been on my mind for many years and until I purchased my Tote 'N Float that's where it stayed. I just didn't have the gumption to pack anything else in there. Now that I have fished the pool it is one of my favorite spots on the river.

The pool is deep, long and the current stays along the cliff wall on the far side. In my boat it is easy to float through the pool while casting dry flies into the ever present foam-line, and then kick back upstream to the head of the pool using my swim fins. Since this water gets very little pressure, it is feasible to fish the pool for several hours without wearing it out.

Besides fishing dry flies in the current along the rock wall the pool is excellent for subsurface patterns, such as nymphs and streamers. Using a heavy sink-tip line you can dredge up chunky fish, mostly rainbows, with the odd brown available.

On my first trip below the dam my partner and I witnessed a brown jump only a few feet from our boat. The trout was two feet long if it was an inch! Although there aren't many browns in

◆

Stimulator patterns do a good job of imitating the adult stonefly. Fishermen should be prepared with an assortment of colors to match the different stonefly hatches.

The Yakima River just below Roza Dam.

◆

Packing a boat down to the section of the river below Roza Dam.

the river the area immediately below the dam is the most likely spot to catch one.

Once you leave the pool it is an easy float to your car parked near the tunnel, but there are several other good stretches of water to fish along the way if you have time. The road veers away from the river just past the tunnel and as you break into the lower valley the river takes on a completely different look. The arid hills of the canyon give way to fertile orchards and scrub willows line the stream as this noble trout stream flows ever closer to it's undignified end.

Selah to the Columbia

ALTHOUGH THERE ARE TROUT IN THE YAKIMA RIVER below Selah, and over the years I have heard stories of some very large fish taken, the numbers start to dwindle the farther downstream you go. So for all practicality the Yakima River as a trout stream is the river from the Easton area down to Selah.

As the river snakes along through the lower valley it becomes dirty and polluted with agricultural and irrigation drainage and becomes too warm to support healthy populations of trout. This lower section of river does contain species like catfish and has a decent smallmouth bass population.

The Yakima brings life all along it's journey, but at a high price. By the time this jewel of central Washington reaches it's confluence with the Columbia River it has widened, slowed and lost all semblance of a blue ribbon trout stream.

Vibrant fall colors in a small pond along the banks of the Yakima.

Tim Irish with a Yakima Canyon rainbow.

Tim Irish, the Yakima's First Trout Guide

*M*Y PHONE RANG EARLY ONE MORNING AND AN excited voice on the other end yelled out "Get yourself over here right now!" I recognized the voice as that of Tim Irish, a long time friend, and the Yakima River's first trout guide. He went on, "I went out to the river yesterday and there are golden stones everywhere. The fish are going nuts!" It didn't take me long to throw my gear in the truck.

It was the first week in March and the first year that the Yakima became a year-round fishery. A few months had passed since I had been on the river and as I drove through blowing snow and winter conditions over Snoqalmie Pass the thought of rising trout on the Yakima River seemed a bit odd.

I met Tim at the Bighorn Access Area at 10 a.m. He had his raft assembled, in the water and within 10 minutes we were heading downstream through the fog in 40 degree weather. We were alone save for two wayward mallards that almost collided with us in the fog.

There were no stonefly adults to be seen so I opted for a Golden Stonefly Nymph. Tim chose a Yellow Stimulator insisting that the fish would still remember the adults. First cast . . . I hung up and lost my nymph. Tim's first cast . . . bam, fish on! We pulled over, Tim landed his fish, and I tied on another fly.

When we resumed our float I cast out, and . . . I hung up and lost my nymph. Tim cast out again and . . . bam, fish on! Well this went on for a couple more fish and finally Tim said, "Why don't you tie on a Stimulator?" and just as he spoke those words, I cast out, hung up and lost my fly. Without faltering Tim continued, "or you could do that."

Well, I did switch to a Stimulator and had my best day on the river. I haven't even come close since. By day's end Tim and I had risen over 140 fish on Yellow Stimulators. The next day we did the same float but it wasn't nearly as good. We only rose 97 fish!

Tim Irish has been guiding on the Yakima River since 1983. While in a popular fly shop in Seattle, Tim mentioned that he was going to start guiding on the Yakima River. They nearly laughed him out the door. There were steelhead, salmon, sturgeon and bass guides in the state, but who on earth would pay to be guided for trout down the Yakima River? Well, as the saying goes, the rest is history. Tim has clients nearly every day of the season now and there are a dozen or so other guides working the river on a regular basis.

Tim and I both grew up in Ellensburg. We graduated from high school together and fished the Yakima River since we were kids—but not together. It wasn't until I became an outdoor writer and Tim became a fishing guide that our rivers crossed ... so to speak. Today Tim and I fish together as often as we can.

Probably no one knows the Yakima River as well as Tim Irish. He is literally on the river every day of the season and knows the water intimately. When you float with Tim he will approach an area, anchor, and say things like, "OK, there's an 18 incher under that branch by that crooked stick" or "over there behind that rock there is a 20 incher, but he's real smart so you have to make a precise presentation to get him to rise." Seldom is he wrong about such matters.

Tim has come up with a leader system to use on the Yakima specifically for casting dry flies into the bank during high water fishing during the summer: 60 percent of the leader is a stiff, .020-mono butt section, 20 percent is half-and-half .015 stiff mono and a .011 medium stiff mono transition and the remaining 20 percent is a soft tippet, either 3X, 4X or 5X depending on the fly used. Total length of the leader is 100 inches. This leader design works perfectly at turning over dries for tight-to-the-bank summer fishing found on the Yakima.

Tim also designs flies to match the specific hatches throughout the season. Naturally, by spending so much time on the river, Tim has experimented with nearly every style of fly pattern available. His designs are culminations of standard and new-wave patterns fine-tuned specifically for the Yakima. It's worth it to take a trip down the river with Tim just so you can heist a few of his flies when he isn't looking.

Most rivers have a gate keeper, so to speak, someone who is snared by it's essence and reveres it's existence. On the Yakima, that gate keeper is Tim Irish.

◆

Tim Irish's favorite Baetis *pattern, tied on a wide gap hook for greater hooking ability.*

A beautiful winter rainbow taken in March on a Yellow Stimulator during a golden stonefly hatch.

Hatches, Flies and the Tackle to Fish Them

A S I MENTIONED, THE BEST FISH ON THE YAKIMA don't come easy. Sure, there are times when it seems you can't go wrong, but overall the Yakima is a technical river. To do well you must be proficient in casting, presentation, reading the water and basic river entomology.

One thing that is certain on the Yakima is the eight month long dry fly season. Exact days that the hatches will occur are impossible to predict due to weather and water conditions.

Following is a summary of major hatches on the river as observed by Tim Irish, in his ten years of guiding the river.

March

In a normal weather year the season kicks off during early March with a hatch of golden stoneflies. This can start at any time from March 1st to the 25th. The key for the hatch is the water temperature reaching 46 to 48 degrees. It will start in the Yakima Canyon first, where the water warms a little faster than the upper river. The stonefly hatch will continue on through mid-April, depending on when it started and what part of the river you are fishing.

Even when there are no adults present the trout remember them and will take an adult pattern with gusto. Any adult golden stonefly design will work, the standard is a size 8 Yellow Stimulator. My favorite is a Yellow Irresistible Temptation, by Spirit River, Inc.

When the fish are onto the "stones", casting your fly to the upstream side of any submerged rock will often produce violent takes. And since this hatch happens when it does, there are a lot of big, pre-spawn rainbows moving around.

The trout are not leader shy when taking a big Stimulator, and since the takes are often very aggressive, a size 3X tippet is advised or you will snap off a lot of fish.

Golden Stonefly Nymphs can also be productive if you can't get the fish to rise. The nymphs should be bounced along the bottom dead-drift into the mouths of the feeding trout.

There are several species of stoneflies in the river and the fish are used to seeing them in a variety of sizes. I only use two different stonefly nymphs, a dark one for darker hatches and a Golden Stonefly Nymph tied in different sizes for this hatch. Nymphs tied in size 8 are an all-around good choice.

Also in March, if the weather becomes warm, and it often does, *Baetis* in size 20 will be a factor during the heat of the day. The hatch won't last long so if you can place yourself over a good *Baetis* bed before it happens, all the better.

If you like nymphing a simple dubbed *Baetis* pupa pattern size 16 or 18 and fished on a 5X tippet can be an important fly just in front of the hatch. Some fishermen I know prefer to nymph the entire hatch and do quite well. A dark olive, soft hackle pattern also works quite well for several of the *Baetis* found in the Yakima as do Hare's Ear, Pheasant Tail or any generic mayfly nymph in appropriate colors.

April

The next significant hatch on the Yakima is the March brown mayfly. This large (size 14 to 12) mayfly hatches around the first part of April to mid-month and ends from the 25th to May 10th, depending on water temperatures. The March browns come off in numbers, but the hatch doesn't last long. While they are on though, March browns cause a significant feeding frenzy. Fish an appropriate pattern on a 3X or 4X tippet.

The Pheasant Tail Nymph does a good job of imitating the nymph of the March brown mayfly. Tied the same size as the adult it is a great fly to use just prior to the hatch of duns. And since the hatch is short lived, occurring only during the heat of day, the nymphal stage of this insect may be more fruitful than the adult, in numbers of fish hooked. Soft hackle patterns are significant for the drowned post-hatch.

Baetis will hatch in April during the warmest part of the day and there can even be a few caddis starting to appear by the end of the month.

May

In May the Yakima River comes to life with multiple hatches. There will still be March browns on the water plus the caddis will be hatching regularly. Sometime during the month there will be four or five different species of caddis hatching. The caddis will be in full-swing by Mothers Day, when the long awaited "Mother's Day Hatch" arrives. Swarms of the American Grannom caddis (olive, size 14) will be coming off and the trout will be going ballistic for them.

A realistic March Brown Mayfly pattern.

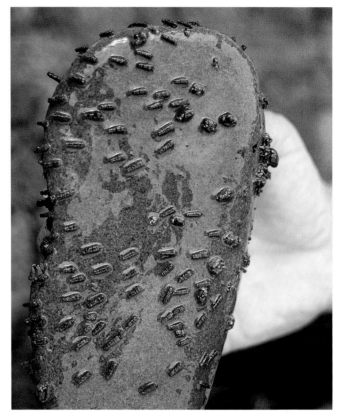

Small caddis cover the rocks in portions of the Yakima. Caddis hatch throughout the spring and summer and are a staple in the diets of Yakima trout.

There will also be little tan short-horned sedge, size 14 and Little Western Weedy-water Sedge, size16. Small Elk Hair Caddis patterns in the appropriate size and color work nicely for matching most caddis hatches. In much of the water, a 3X tippet will suffice, but for particularly slack water a 4X or even 5X tippet may be required. You might even have to switch to a more exact caddis imitation such as a Para-Caddis or an emerger for extremely spooky fished-over trout.

Pale morning dun mayflies also make their appearance by mid- to late-May and last through June and sometimes into July. Thorax duns or parachute PMD's size 16 to 18 are good choices. Fine tippets of 4X or even 5X are needed for proper presentation. Trout may start on the PMD's during the midst of another hatch and if you want to catch fish have a few PMD's in your fly box.

And again, the *Baetis* will be hatching, but now you will see them on the cooler, cloudy days along with the other insects.

Sometimes the biggest problem in May is deciding just which insect the trout are feeding on. There may be several insects hatching at the same time while the trout will be only feeding on one particular stage of one insect.

June

June is another frenzied month on the Yakima. The PMD's will be going all month, heavier early on but continuing throughout the month and into the first part of July.

Caddis will be available in numbers and particularly abun-

Ray Pelland working a stretch of the Yakima Canyon from his pontoon boat.

dant during evening hours. A size 16 Elk Hair Caddis in dark olive is a good choice for the evening rise. However, the trout are very used to seeing caddis by now and a caddis imitation in size 12 or 14 in brown or olive is a good choice for pounding the banks during the day.

Yellow Sallys are prolific in certain areas, especially the upper river. Using a small (size 14) yellow Stimulator or bright yellow Elk Hair Caddis (size 12) will do the trick.

Baetis will again be important during June but you can expect them to appear on the cooler days, especially days that are cloudy, or during those rare days when a June shower passes through

July

Early July finds PMD's still in the picture as well as yellow Sallys. Caddis, again are effective fished throughout the day and major hatches occur during evenings and on into the night.

Baetis again make an appearance but only on the coldest of days or when it rains.

The biggest news during July, and the long awaited event of the season, is the hopper fishing that develops as July progresses. Trout take hopper patterns with the same enthusiasm that they hit adult stoneflies. Hopper patterns tied in size 10 or 12 work fine.

Other terrestrials like ants, bees and beetles are effective

and like hopper patterns should be cast in tight against streamside vegetation.

August

August sees the continuation of the hoppers and is probably the best all-around month to fish them. Caddis put on their evening and night show just like in July and the *Baetis* show only on cold, rainy days, which are rare in August.

One of the best methods in August, because of high water, is to drift the river casting hoppers or large attractors such as a Royal Trude, size 10 or 12, into the banks, except, of course, during the evening and night when caddis are swarming.

September

If ever there was a stream made for September, the Yakima River is it. The water drops during the second week of the month and the river once again becomes wadable from Easton to Roza and beyond. The weather is cooling by now, and combined with great hatches this has become the Yakima's most popular month.

Caddis hatches and terrestrials continue through mid-month, and by then *Baetis* hatches should be in full swing as water temperatures cool continuing through October. If the weather and water are exceptionally warm the hatch can be delayed. A hatch of October caddis comes off from September

Paragliders, slightly off course, descending to the canyon floor.

10th to the 30th, mostly in the upper river. A size 8 Orange Stimulator or any October caddis pattern can produce some exciting fishing if you encounter a hatch of these large caddisflies.

September also hosts a hatch of stoneflies, dirty-cream, size 6, between September 10th and the 30th. This hatch causes a frenzy and the fish remember the adults long after they are gone.

October

Depending largely on how quick and how hard fall invades eastern Washington, the fishing in October can be nearly as good as September. Autumn days are usually warm with temperatures in the 50s and 60s and crisp, frosty nights.

Hatches are mostly *Baetis*, with the blue wing olives stealing the show each afternoon as the water temperatures warm to 48 to 52 degrees. Typical hatches occur from 11 a.m. to 4 p.m. and shorten as the month progresses. The BWO's are size 18 and 20 and fishing them becomes increasingly technical as fall moves on.

Tippets must be fine and casts, presentations and flies must be painstakingly accurate.

There is also a significant hatch of Light Cahills (size 14) that appear from October 1st to the 15th, and often show at the same time as the BWO hatch. Trout often interrupt their BWO feeding to sip in the big mayflies and return to the BWO's when the hatch is over.

November, December, January and February

About the only hatches found in November, December, January and February are midges. There may be a few sporadic Baetis hatches found early in November but the fishing quickly fades out as water temperatures in the river drop below the 40 degree mark.

Trout can be taken during these months but their feeding patterns have slowed with their metabolism and it is only during brief periods each day that trout respond to the fly.

This time of year the Yakima is not fished much for trout. It is whitefish that get attention during cold months and for those

Brilliant fall foliage along the banks of the Yakima River.

A perfect match: Sculpin on the left and the fly to imitate it—the Spuddler.

who are into this type of fishing the Yakima is a good destination.

This is by no means an all-inclusive account of the year's hatches found on the Yakima River. There are many other minor hatches that the fly fisher can certainly experience and on the Yakima matching the hatch is often essential. Then again, there is always the time when a non-specific attractor comes along and works! However, this list covers most hatches and dries and nymphs that imitate these insects will most often produce well.

Tackle

For the spring and summer flows of the Yakima, and with the incessant winds during the spring and early summer, a nine-foot fast-action five to seven-weight rod is a good choice.

During low water periods of fall three and four-weight rods are a better choice.

A weight-forward or double-taper floating line is used most, however if you want to get down with a streamer in deeper pools a heavy sink-tip should be included in your arsenal.

Leaders are largely personal choice but if you plan on float fishing, I would recommend Tim Irish's leader described in a previous section of this journal.

Neoprene waders are best for most of the season, but during July and August air temperatures in Ellensburg and down in the canyon can be unbearably hot. Many anglers choose to wade wet during this time. Felt-soled boots are recommended.

Although this area gets little moisture it will rain unless you bring rain gear and a warm sweater or fleece jacket is a must during every month on the river. When the wind comes up it can get cold in a hurry.

Suggested Fly Patterns

Dries

Yellow Stimulator, Orange Stimulator, Slate Gray Stimulator, Dirty-Cream Stimulator, Irresistable Temptations, Tan Elk Hair Caddis, Olive Elk Hair Caddis, Brown Elk Hair Caddis, Hi-Vis Para-Caddis, March Brown, Mahogany Dun, Gray Drake, Pale Morning Dun, Green Drake, Grey Dun, Adams, Blue Wing Olive, Black *Baetis*, Light Cahill, Royal Trude, hoppers, ants and beetles.

Nymphs

Prince Nymph, Gold-Ribbed Hare's Ear, Pheasant Tail, Dark Stonefly, Golden Stonefly, Black Rubberleg, Emerging Caddis, Brassie, Dark Midge Pupa.

Streamers

Spuddler, Muddler, Olive Zonker, Marabou Muddler, Black Woolly Bugger, Woolhead Sculpins.

Small nymph patterns useful for fishing the Yakima.

Winter fishing on the Yakima.

Fall colors along the upper river.

The Future

*I*N THE TEN YEARS SINCE TIM IRISH FLOATED HIS FIRST client down the Yakima the river has undergone many changes for the better. As with many rivers around the country, increased use of the resource and increased public awareness eventually resulted in a catch-and-release, wild fish success story. The Yakima has evolved into a top-rated trout stream.

Over the years through magazine articles, word-of-mouth and the general increased interest in fly fishing, pressure on the Yakima has grown. Where once you found only an old pick-up or two parked along the river down in the Yakima Canyon, now, during summer you find expensive vehicles crammed into every available wide-spot along the canyon road. Fishing is seldom crowded though, at least not like that found on some of the more popular western rivers. You can always find some solitude on the Yakima without too much effort.

Sometimes those of use who grew up along the banks of the Yakima feel threatened and overwhelmed by all the "foreigners" invading "our water". Each season brings more people. It's normal to have a possessive connection to home water and everyone must feel that way about someplace. But all home water, whether it be yours or somebody else's needs friends, lots of them.

All you have to do is look around and you will see resources in dire need of a few friends. Through numbers we can make changes and protect the future of our resources. There have been so many blatant violations of nature over the past several decades that we must protect what we have left.

Since the white man came to the Yakima River he has given little regard to the river and the life within. He has used the water and land to serve his own needs, often with reckless abandon for all else. The anadromous fish of the river system are all but gone. They can never be replaced with fish of hatchery origin. The Yakima is not unique in this matter. Many rivers have suffered such wrongs and are in desperate need of friends. Some have been saved, many have been lost.

In the last decade the trout fishery in the Yakima has become blue ribbon quality. It has made a comeback from near disaster. It now has a strong following—many fly fishing friends, who united as a group have a strong voice in what the future holds for this water. A voice that will hopefully keep improving all aspects of this valuable resource and it's fine trout fishing; a voice that will not accept a breach of nature imposed by modern man. It is your voice. Let it be heard.

◆

A beautiful rainbow from the area below Roza Dam.

The City of Ellensburg, Where to Stay, Guide Services, Fly Shops and other Useful Information

*I*N 1870, A. J. SPAWN MOVED A SMALL CABIN TO THE banks of Wilson Creek in the Kittitas Valley and opened a trading post. The trading post became known as Robbers' Roost and a settlement was born. In 1872 the store, along with a 160 acre land claim, was sold to a man named John Shoudy. Shoudy plotted a town site and named it after his wife, Mary Ellen. Thus the town of Ellensburg was born.

The railroad came, the town thrived, and plans to make Ellensburg the state capital were thwarted when most of the downtown was destroyed in a fire on July 4, 1889. The city was rebuilt and later became the county seat as well as the home for Central Washington University.

The biggest claim to fame for Ellensburg is the nationally famous Ellensburg Rodeo which began in 1923. This event is held each Labor Day weekend and draws contestants and wanna-be cowboys from around the nation.

Being centrally located along the Yakima River, Ellensburg is the most practical resting spot for visiting fishermen. There are numerous motels, restaurants, bed and breakfasts, etc.

There is a KOA campground located along the Yakima River near the West I-90 Interchange, Rt 1 Box 252, Ellensburg, WA 98926, (509) 925-9319. Camping and R.V. spaces are also available at the River View campground, 15 miles south of Ellensburg on Highway 821, (509) 952-6043. Rustic camping can also be found in the canyon.

Local guide services include: Irish's Guide Service, 308 S. Pearl, Ellensburg, WA 98926, (509) 925-3588; The Evening Hatch, P.O. Box 1295, Ellensburg, WA 98926, (509) 962-5959; Charles Cooper, Ellensburg, WA. 98926, (509) 962-2682; Gary's Fly Shoppe and Yakima River Outfitters, 1210 West Lincoln, Yakima, WA 98902, (509) 457-FISH.

In addition to local guides several of the fly shops in the Seattle-Tacoma area offer guided trips on the river.

Fly fishing supplies and flies can be purchased at the following places: Kittitas County Trading Co., 103 N. Main, Ellensburg, WA 98926, (509) 925-1109; Outdoor Store, 413 N. Main, Ellensburg, WA 98926, (509) 962-3587; River View Campground (flies only), (509) 952-6043; and in Yakima, Gary's Fly Shoppe, 1210 West Lincoln, Yakima, WA 98902, (509) 457-FISH.

◆

A trout rises in the slack water just above Roza Dam.

For additional information on the Ellensburg area, services or guides contact: Ellensburg Chamber of Commerce, 436 N. Sprague St., Ellensburg, WA 98926, (509) 925-3137.

There is little written about the Yakima River and it's fishing. As of this writing there are two sources which may prove useful if you are planning a trip. They are: Recreational Users' Map of The Yakima River, produced by the Kittitas County Field & Stream Club, P.O. Box 522, Ellensburg, WA 98926; and Fly Fishing Video Magazine's Washington State's Yakima River Trout, by Jim & Kelly Watt, Producers/Hosts, 22075 SE 61st, Issaquah, WA 98027, (800) 327-2893.

Proposed Salmon Hatchery

*W*HEN GEORGE B. McCLELLAN EVENTUALLY ARRIVED at the lakes near Snoqualmie Pass the Yakima River system was beaming with salmon and steelhead. A passage from his journal of 1853 reads: "In all the lakes except the small ones on the divide & Willailootzas are found salmon and trout; canoes are carried up the river to those lakes, & the best fisheries are either on or near the lake. In Willailootzas some large fish & probably they are not salmon. It is a circumstance worthy of note that these lakes, in the very heart of the mountains, should be accessible to canoes & salmon." The days of salmon teeming in the upper Yakima are long gone.

Congress established the Northwest Power Planning Council to develop a program to, in part, protect and enhance the Columbia Basin's fish and wildlife.

The once prolific wild salmon runs of the Yakima River and many other Columbia River tributaries are gone. There are several reasons for this. Hydroelectric and irrigation dams, commercial fishing, poor logging, mining and livestock grazing practices, excessive irrigation draw-downs and unscreened water diversions—they all took a toll.

Hatcheries were designed as a solution but ended up contributing to the problem by introducing fish with inferior genes prone to disease and with poor survival and reproductive abilities. Hatcheries along the Columbia system became a "put a bandaid on the problem" solution. The anadromous fish runs on many streams ultimately lost.

There are some who believe that salmon and steelhead should be reintroduced to the Yakima River system to supplement the dwindling stocks of anadromous fish that return each year. As of this writing a salmon hatchery on the upper Yakima River has been proposed. Native Americans are largely behind this effort. Some tribes are guaranteed the right to fish for Columbia salmon by treaties with the United States dating back to 1855.

You can't fish for what's not there. A salmon hatchery on the upper Yakima would almost certainly put more fish of hatchery origin back in the river, but at what price?

Just as there are those who believe the salmon should be reintroduced, there are others who believe that we should leave well-enough alone, that putting salmon back in the upper

A box of the authors favorite streamer patterns for fishing some of the larger pools and runs on the Yakima.

Yakima will only hurt the trout populations and eventually ruin the fishery.

The fear is juvenile salmon would compete for food with the native trout that have been nurtured over the years to create the blue ribbon trout fishery.

Nobody can dispute that the loss of the Yakima's salmon was a sad development in the river's history. Is the reintroduction of hatchery salmon worth the possible destruction of the success story of the wild trout fishery? Most trout fishermen think not.

The hatchery issue is far from settled and those with an opinion should let it be known. Appropriate places to voice your view on this issue would be: Washington Trout, P.O. Box 402 Duval, Washington 98019; Northwest Power Planning Council, 851 S.W. Sixth Ave., Suite 1100, Portland, OR 97204; The Yakima Indian Nation P.O. Box 151 Toppenish, Washington 98948; and the Washington Department of Wildlife, Fisheries Management Division, 600 Capitol Way North, Olympia, WA 98501-1091.

Irresistible Temptation Olive   Irresistible Temptation Yellow   Irreisistible Temptation Orange
Irresistible Stimulator Olive   Stimulator Slate Gray   Stimulator Dirty-Cream   Dave's Hopper
SRI Superior Stone Fly   Western Stonefly Brown   Stonefly Black   Bead Head G.R.H.E.   Brassie
Standard Prince   Flashback Pheasant Tail   Midge Pupa   S.R. Woolhead Sculpin Olive
Woolly Bugger Black   Woolly Bugger Olive   Woolly Bugger Brown

Hi-Vis Para-Cricket   Hi-Vis Foam Ant   Yellow Jacket   Yellow Sally
CDC Elk Caddis Brown   CDC Elk Caddis Olive   CDC Elk Caddis Dun   Royal Coachman Trude
March Brown   Standard Light Cahill   Gray Wulff   Mahogany Dun Thorax   Standard Adams
Gray Drake Extended Comparadun   Gray Dun Extended Comparadun   Blue Wing Olive Extended Comparadun
Tan Extended Comparadun   Standard P.M.D. Comparadun
Crystal Parachute Midge Adult Black   CDC Emerger   No Hackle B W O   Hi-Vis Para-Caddis Olive   Hi-Vis Para-Caddis Tan

A colorful rainbow from the Yakima River taken in the Ellensburg area.

Summary

The sun has been below the canyon wall for some time now. As the light dims in the western sky, the air becomes thick with caddis dancing their song of love. The water in the tail-out looks as though it is raining; trout, being the opportunists they are, gorge themselves on the abundant caddis. Trout after trout is caught in those last moments of light before calling it quits. Even then walking from the river, the fading sound of fish rising can be heard all the way to the car. The pesky caddisflies crawl all over you as you struggle with waders and stow your gear. And as you drive along the river towards home you notice your face muscles sore from grinning. It has been a good day.

As the writing of this journal draws to a close I have many visions of the Yakima River floating in my mind: fish caught, fish lost, friends made and oodles of trivia from past seasons on the river. Like the time several years ago when we misjudged the length of a float down the upper river during the fall and ended up floating an hour or so in the dark. My dad was along on this trip and he was a bit uneasy about the situation. We nearly fell out of the boat, doubled over with laughter, when my friend Ken responded to my dad's anxiety with: "Don't worry Cecil, at least now we don't have to keep watching for those rocks and snags."

The Yakima River, like all great rivers, means many things to many people. It brings life to a very large agricultural region of Washington state. It was once revered by Native Americans for it's plentiful salmon and steelhead and is now a destination for fly fishermen from around the west.

It is awkward to associate such a magnificent natural resource like the Yakima River with money. But associated it is, from the crops, orchards and rangelands it nurtures to the revenues from recreational users of which anglers are a large part.

It is in everyones best interest to make sure that the purity and integrity of the river continues. We simply can not let the greed of a few destroy what is left. Hopefully, the upper Yakima, filled with wild trout will last for decades to come.